Cool MOM Quotes coloring book

We hope you enjoy this book!

Show us your creations and support our small, independent business by leaving us a review on Amazon

This
cool mom
is called

_ _ _ _ _ _ _ _ _ _ _ _ _ _ _ _ _

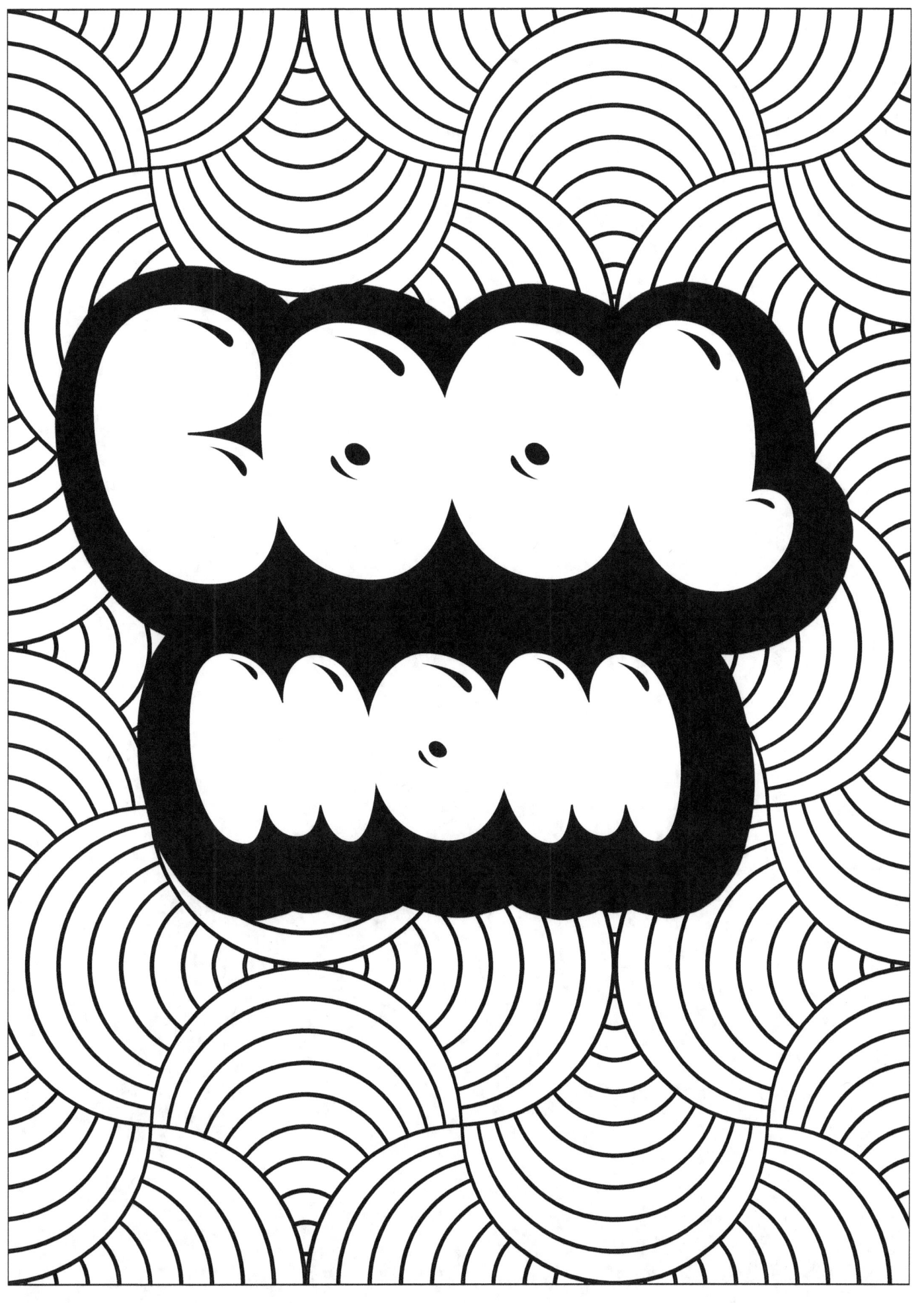

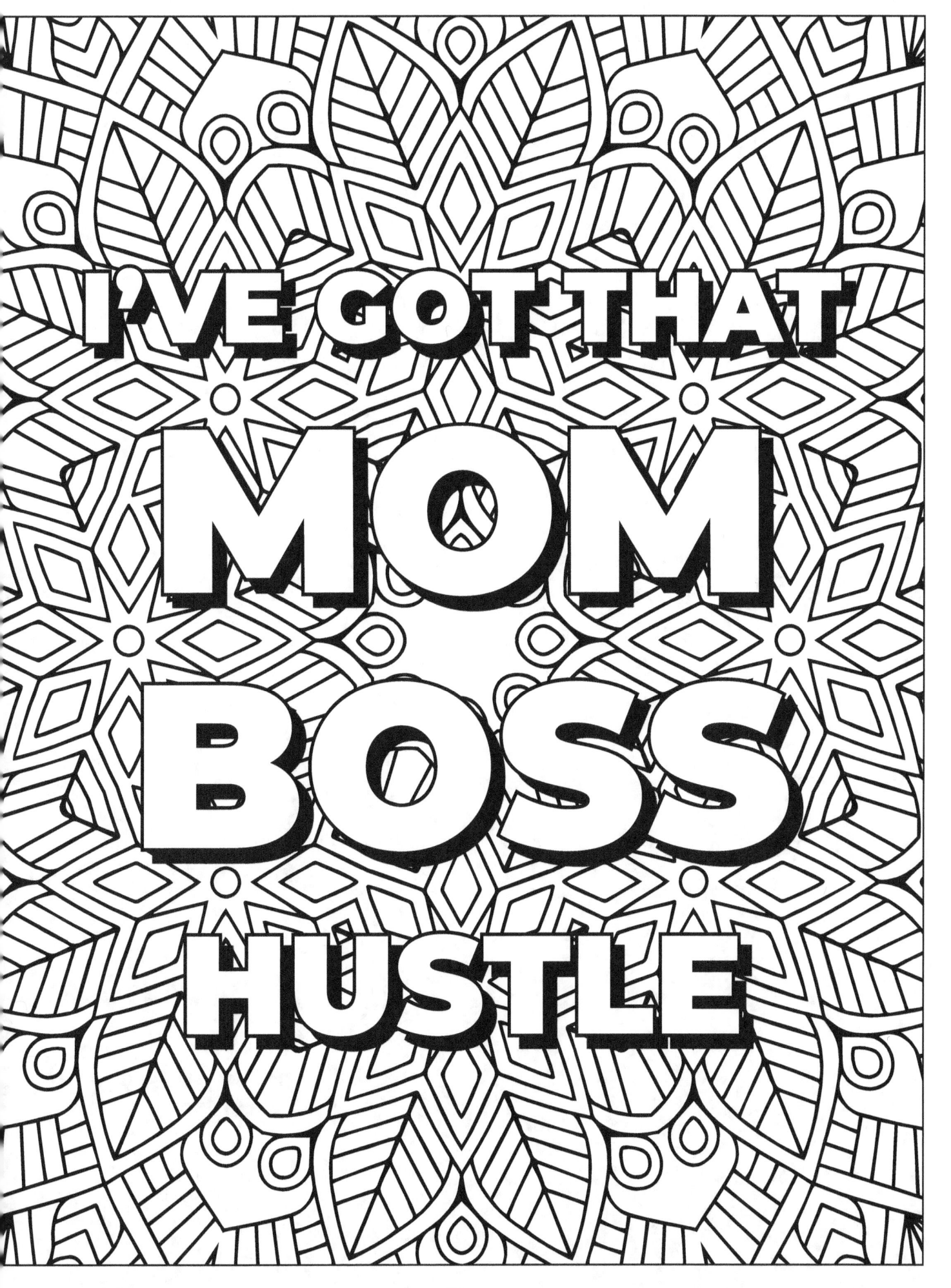

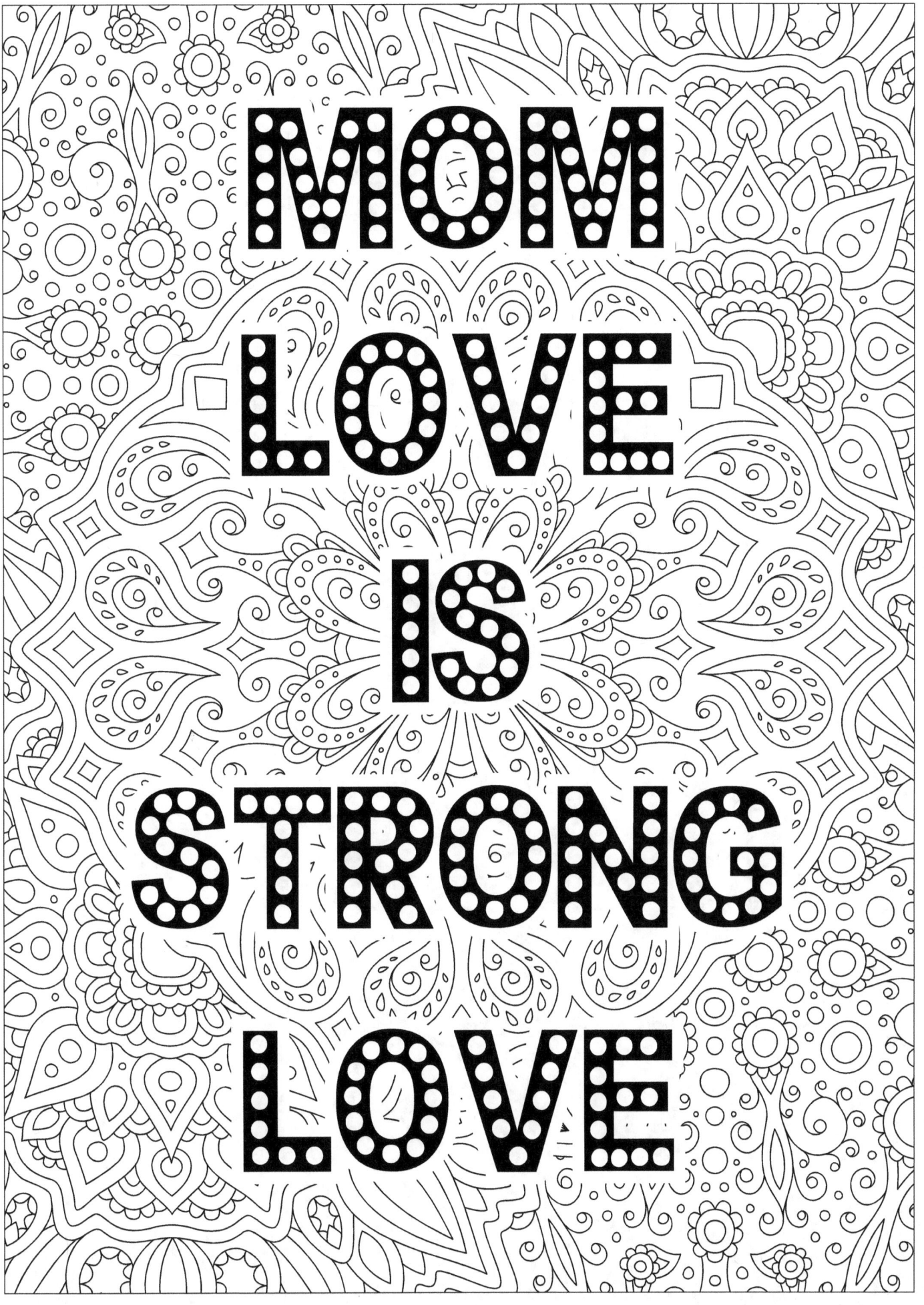

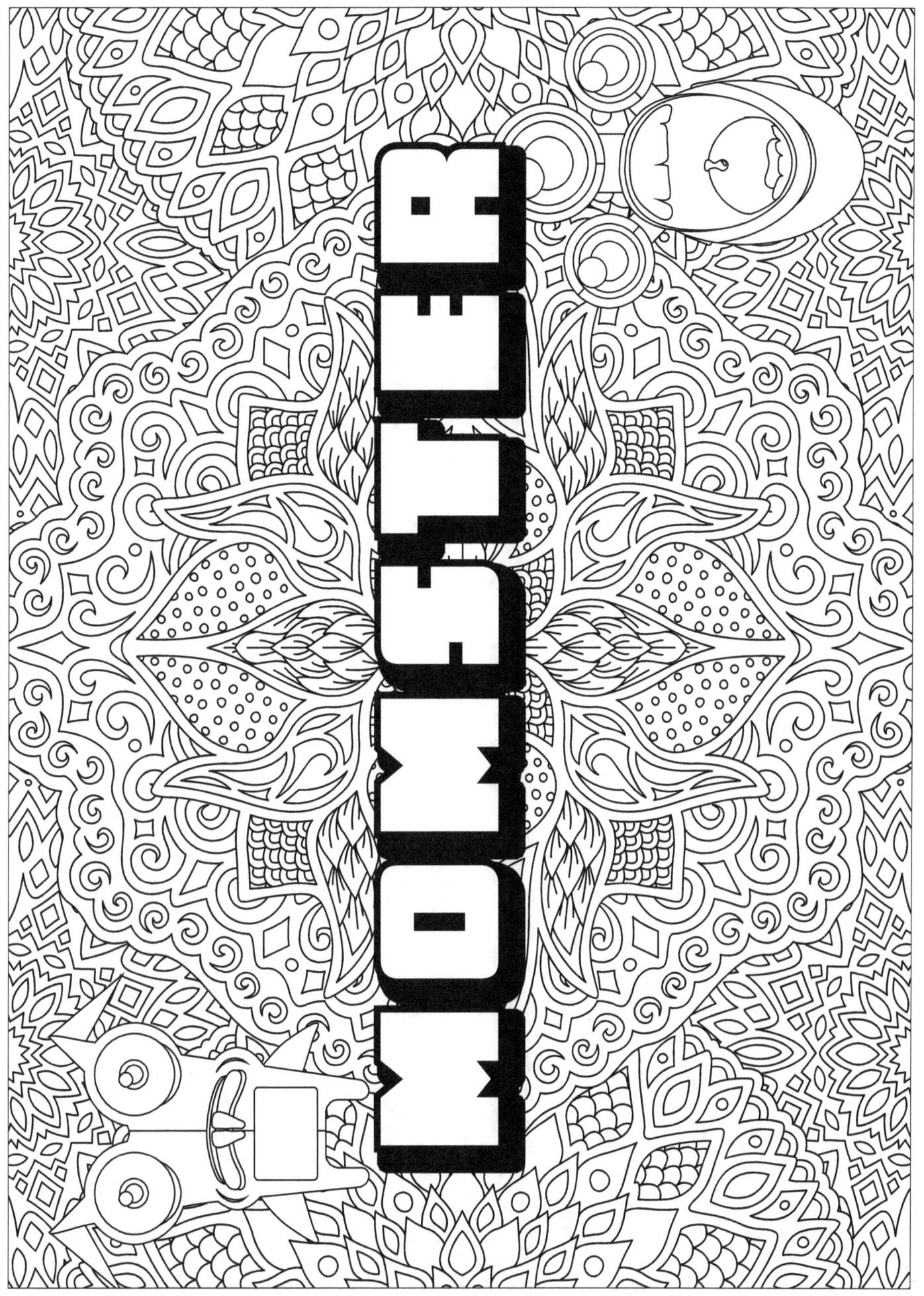

FINDER OF ALL THINGS

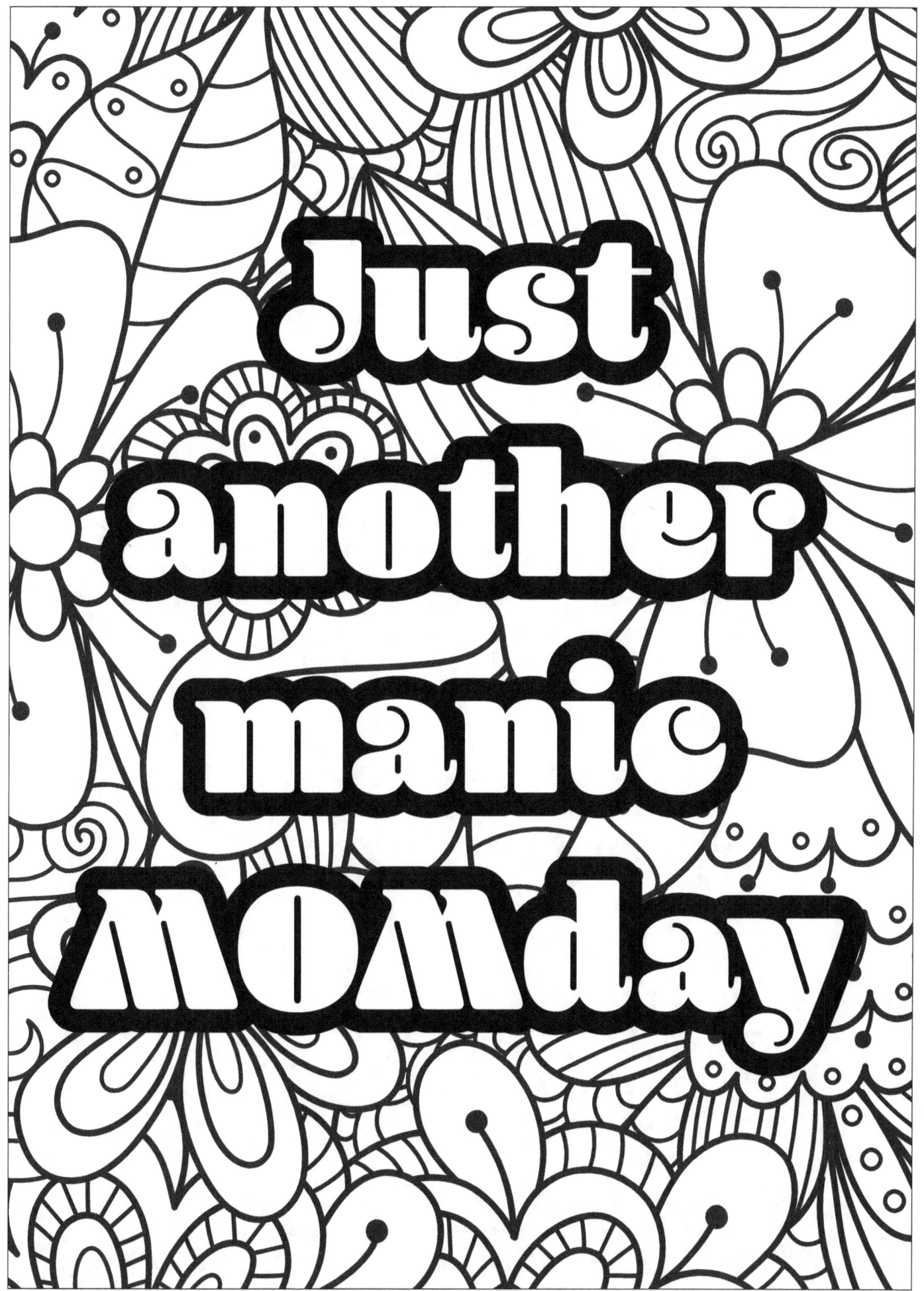

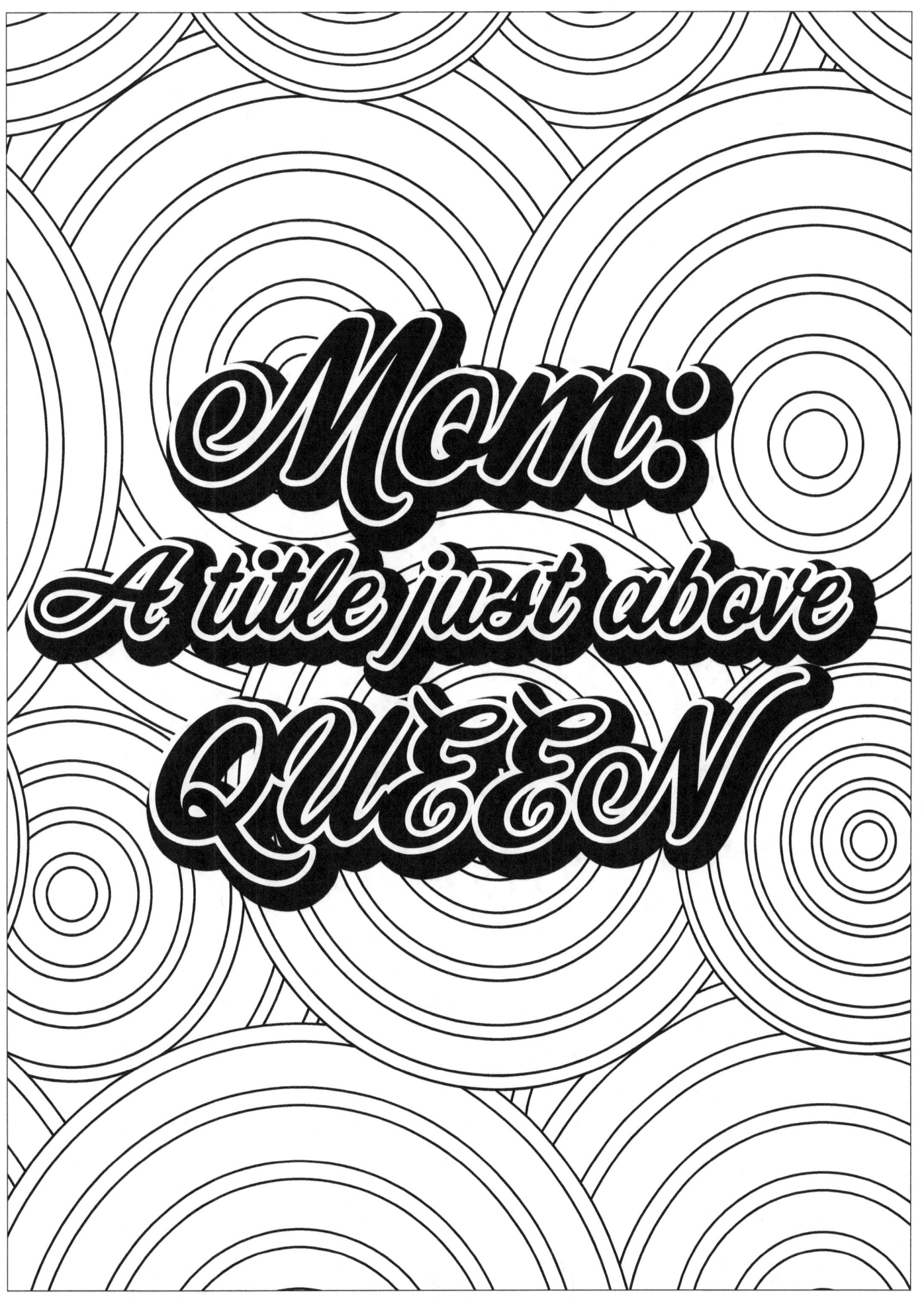

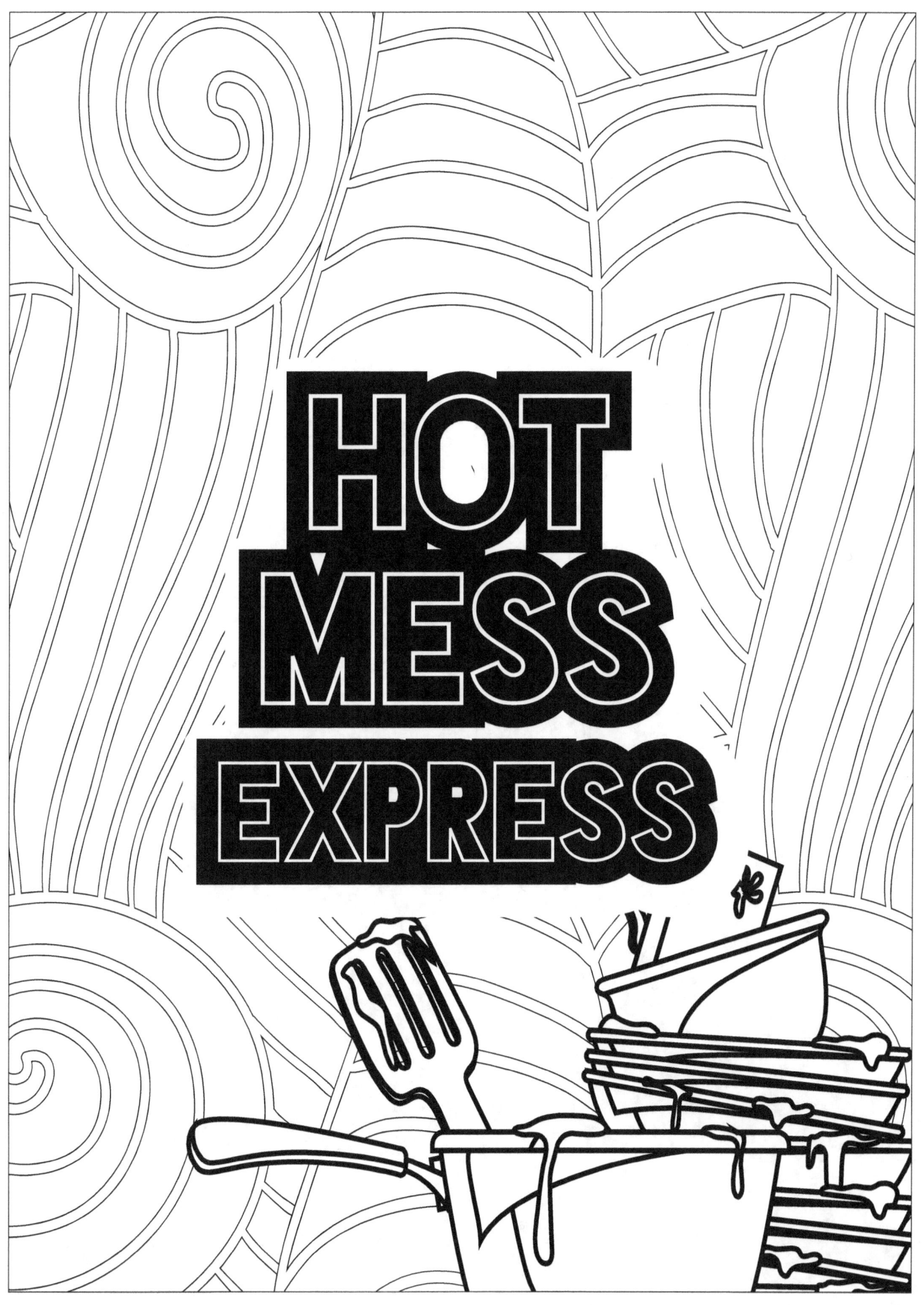

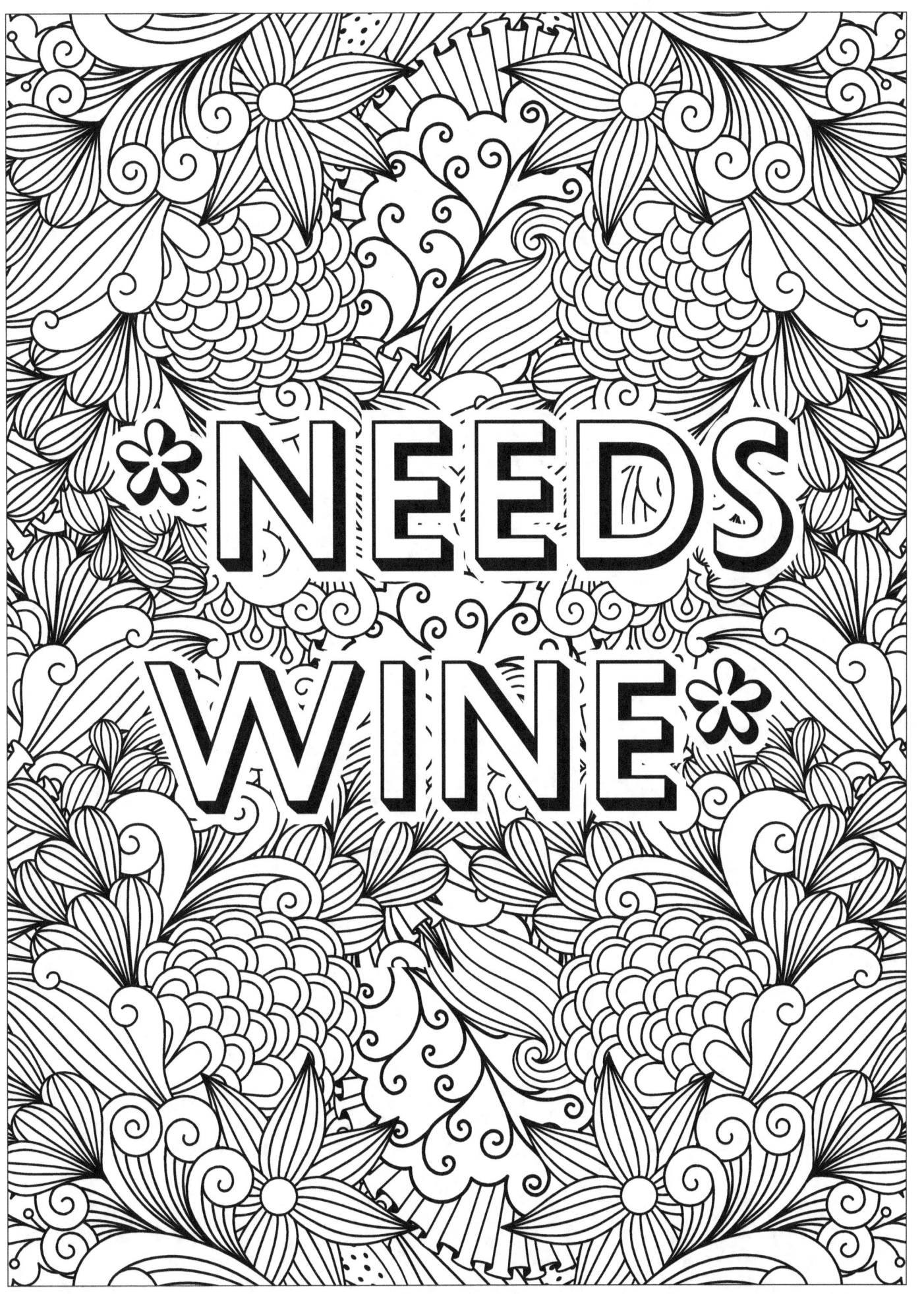

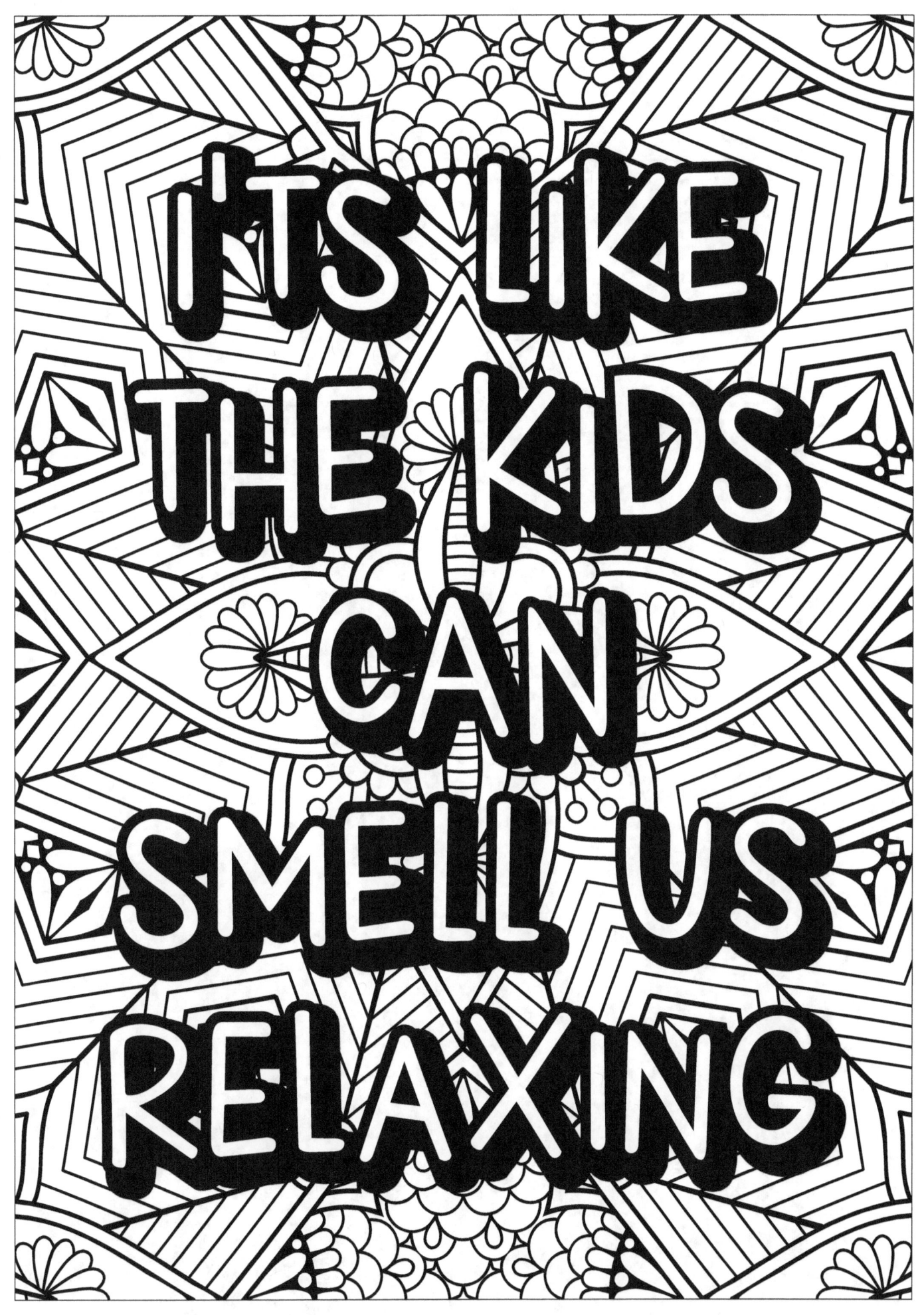

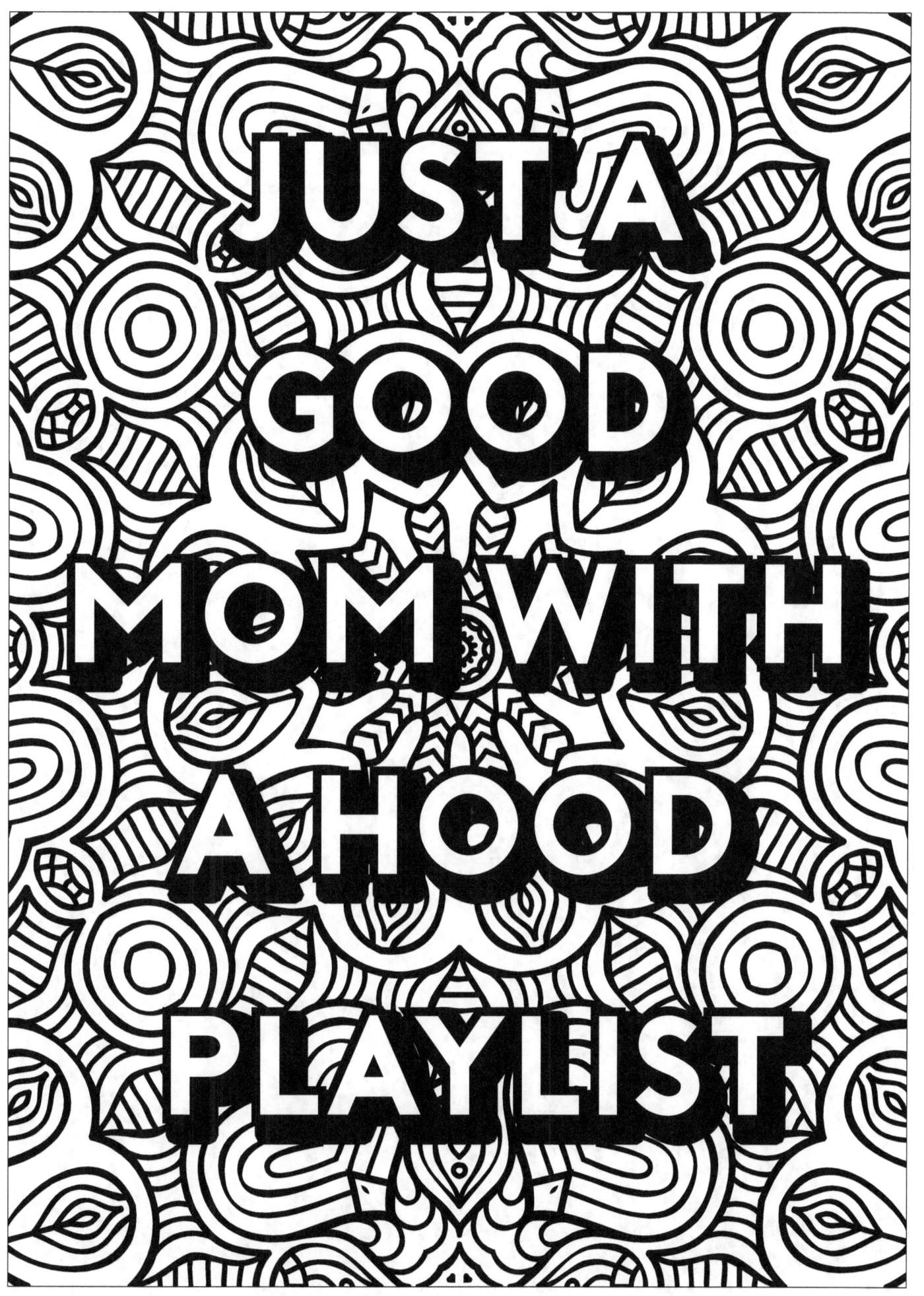

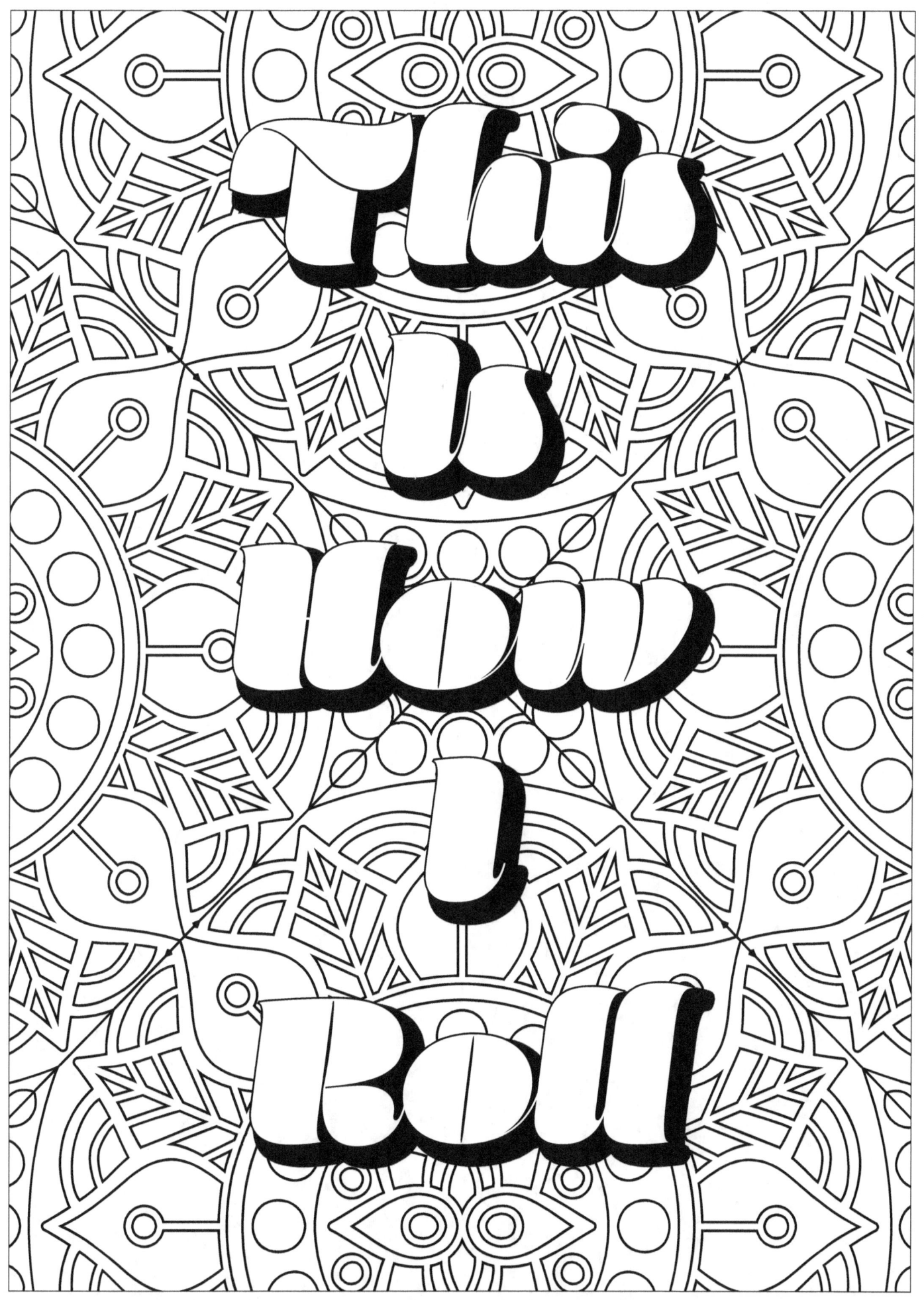

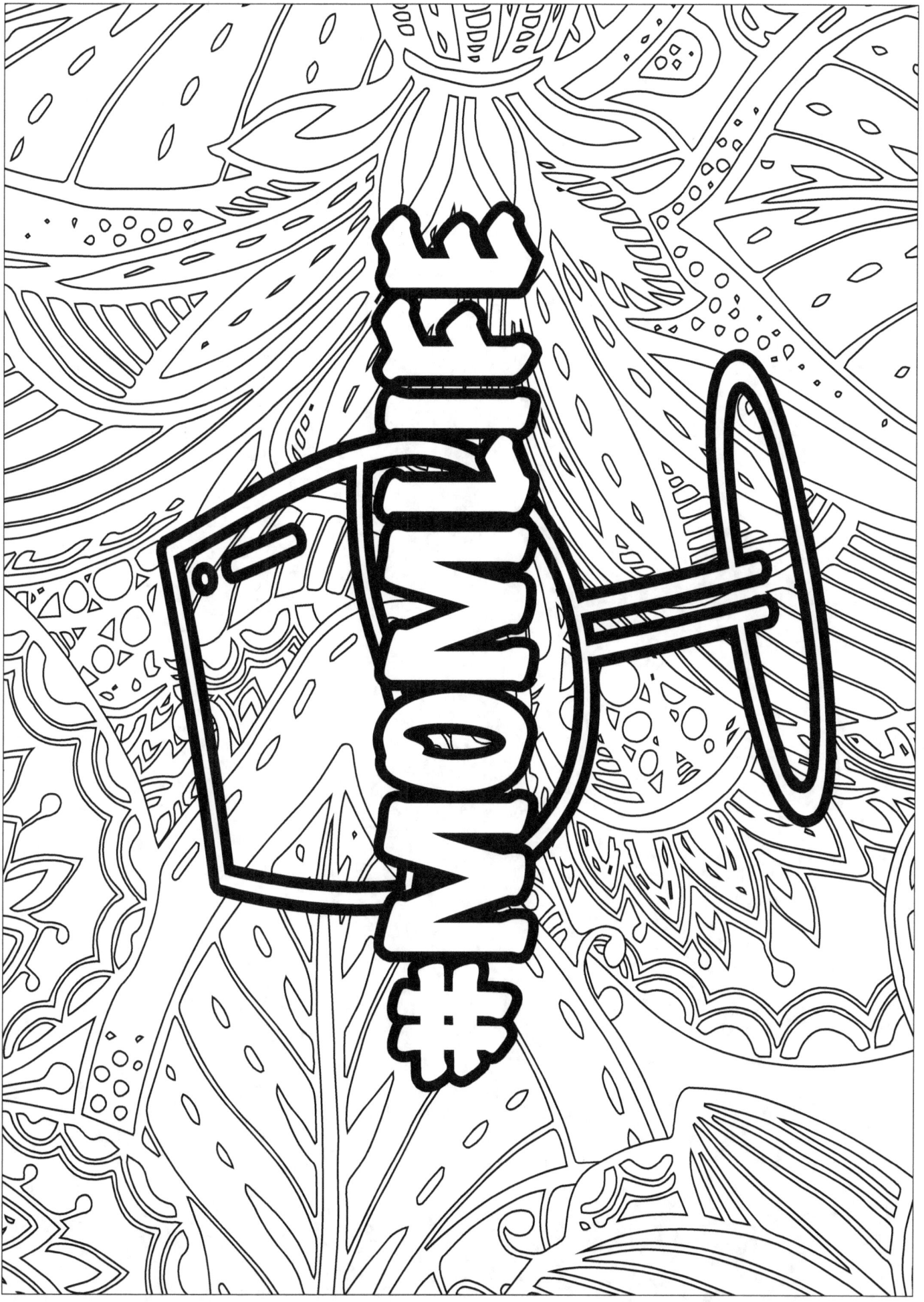

HUSTLE LIKE A MOTHER

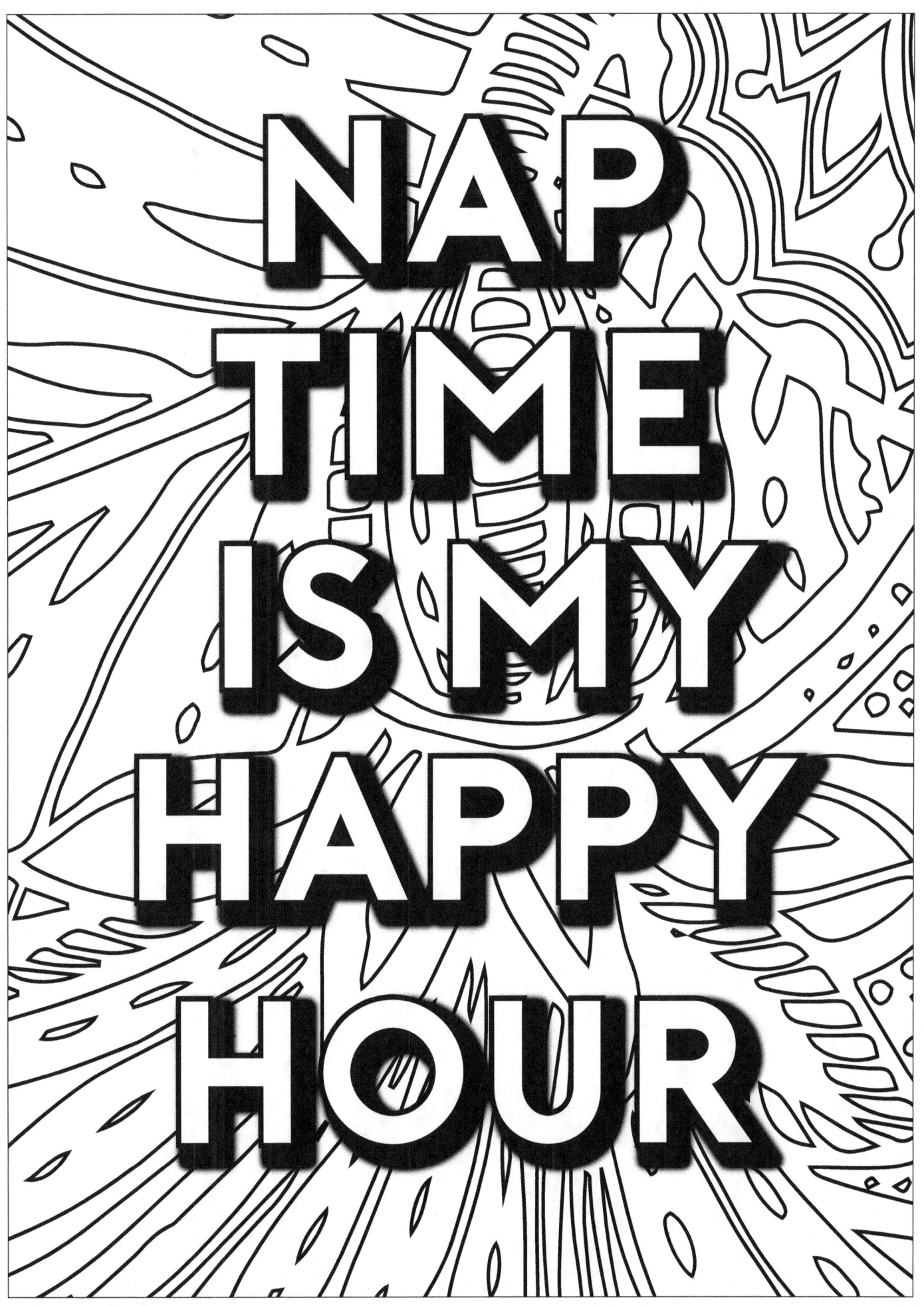

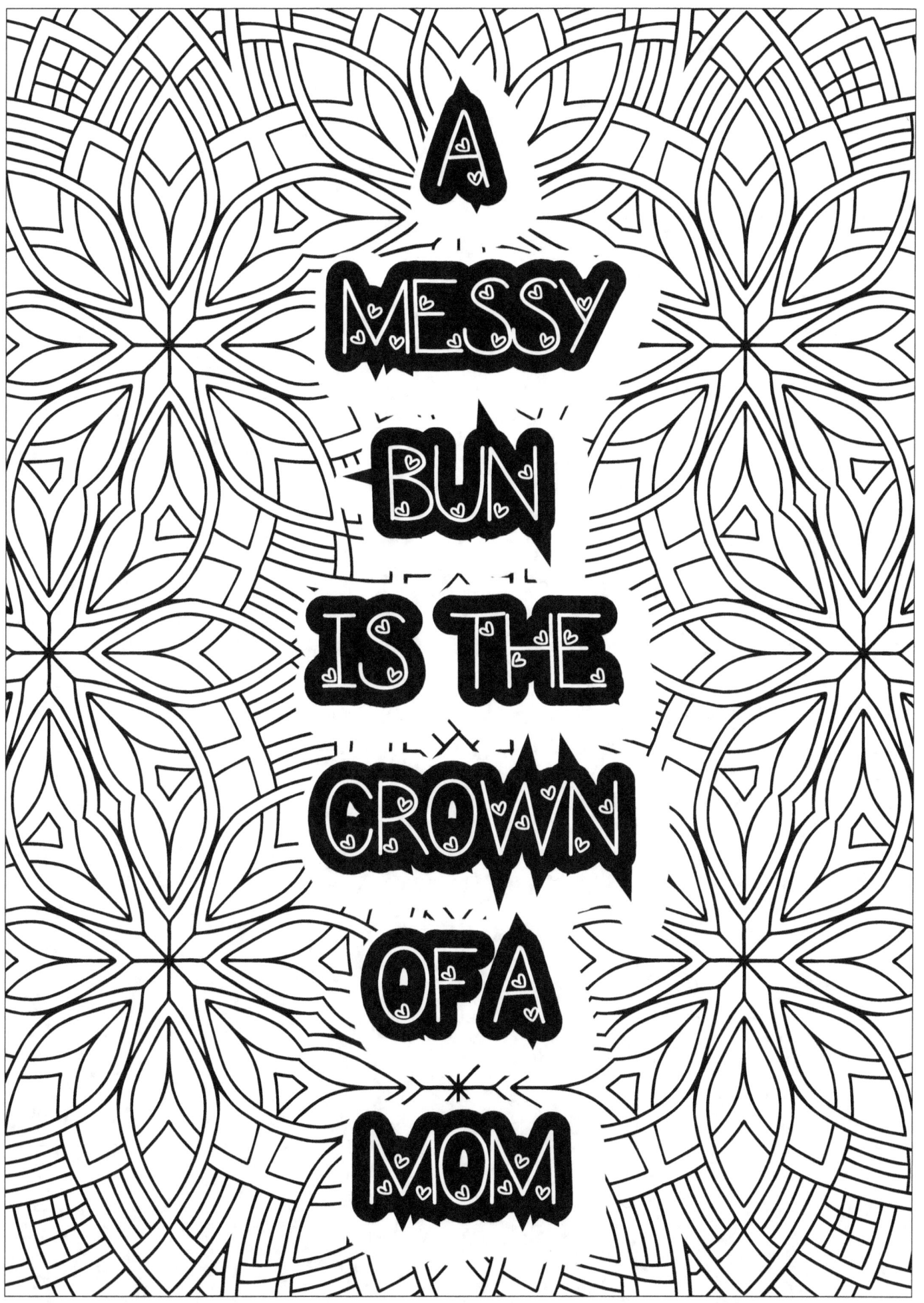

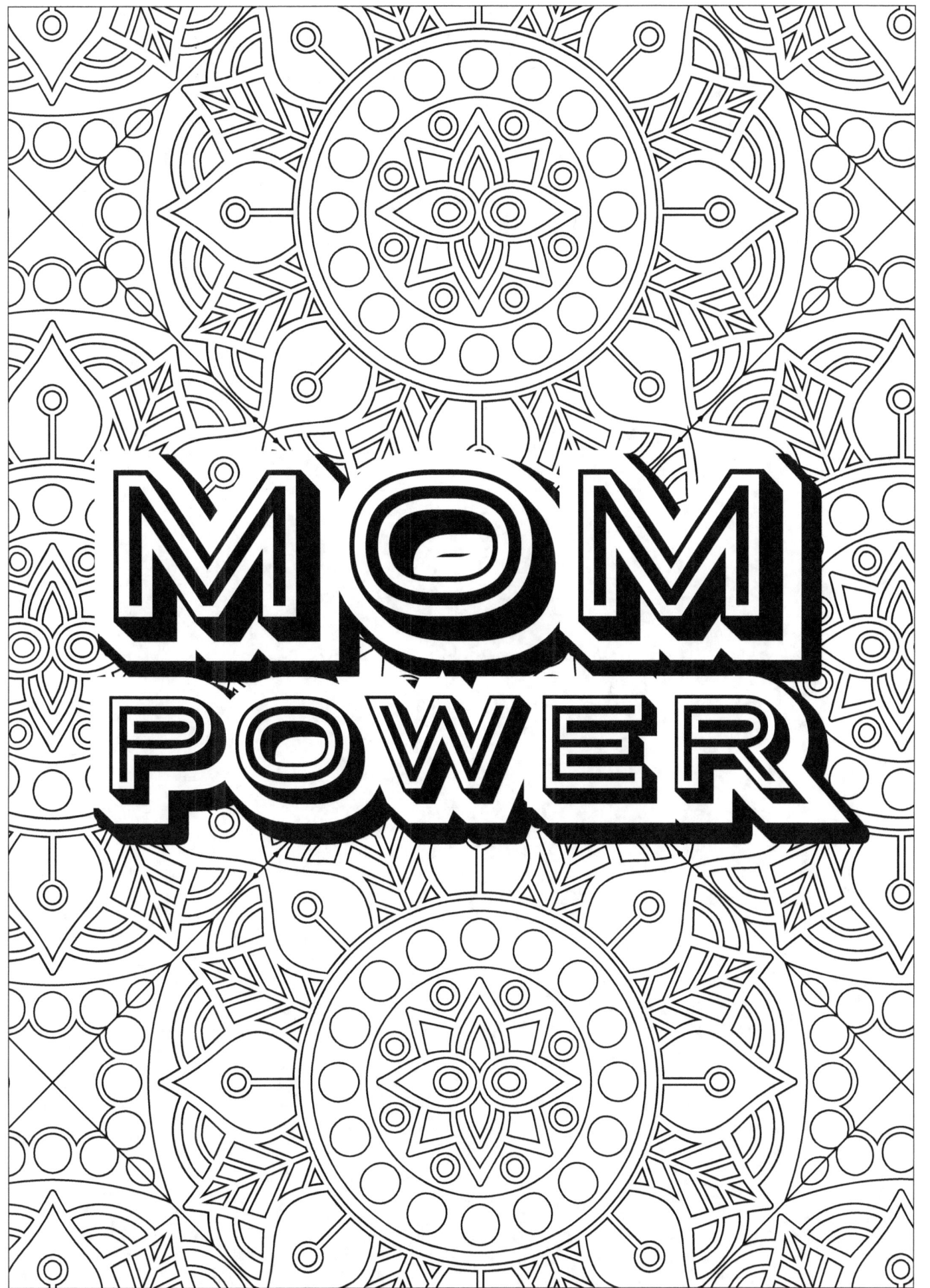

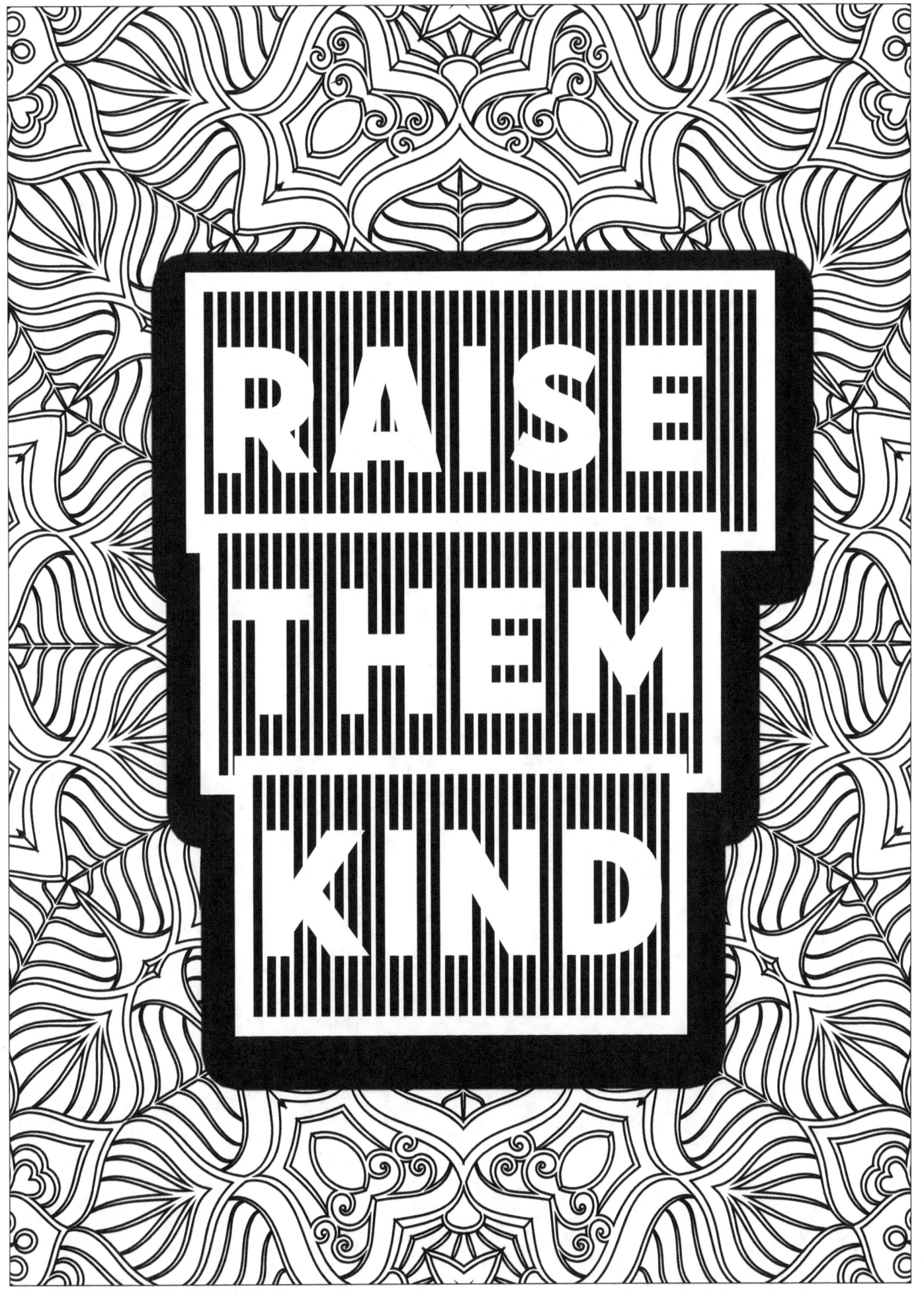

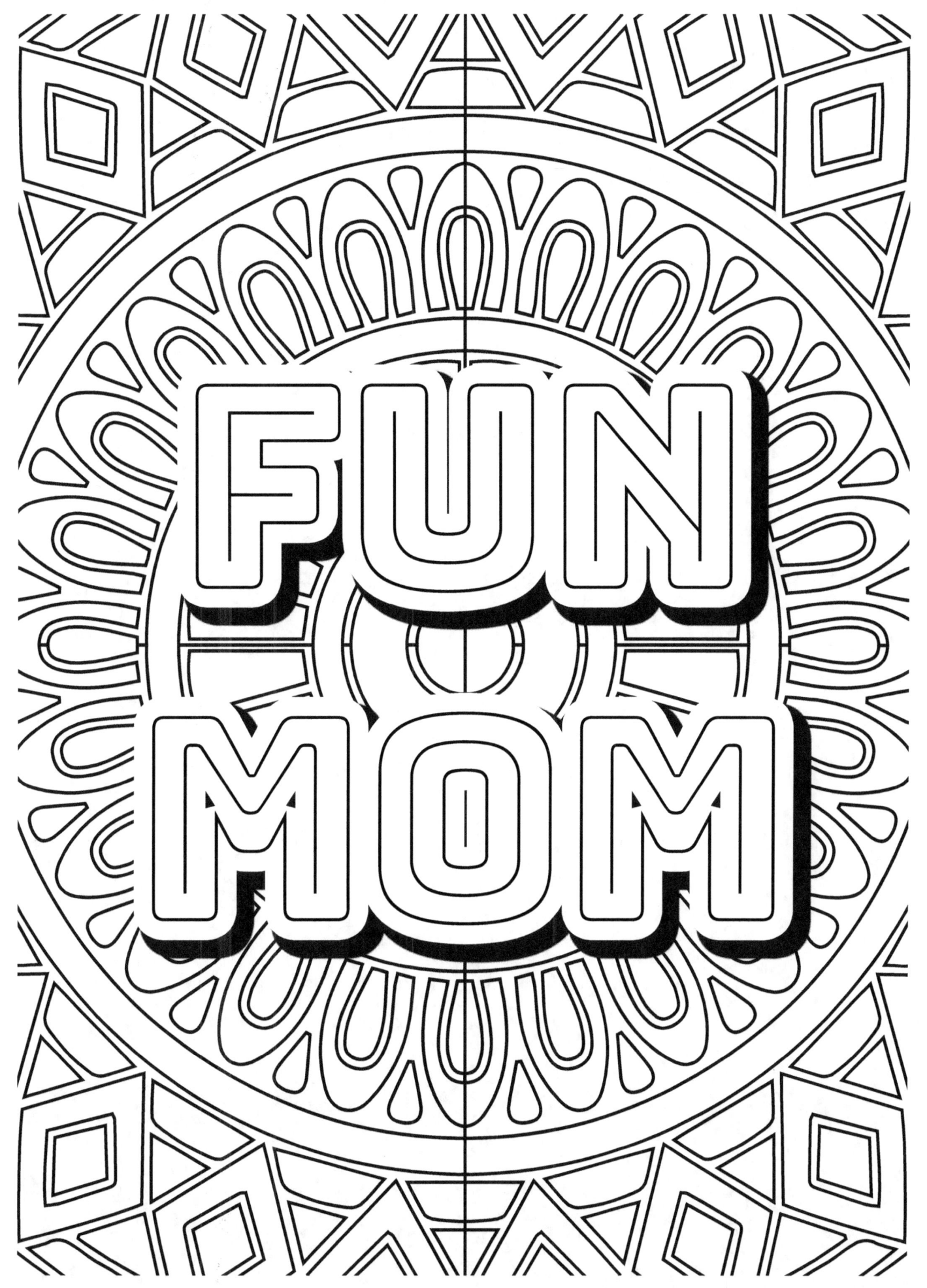

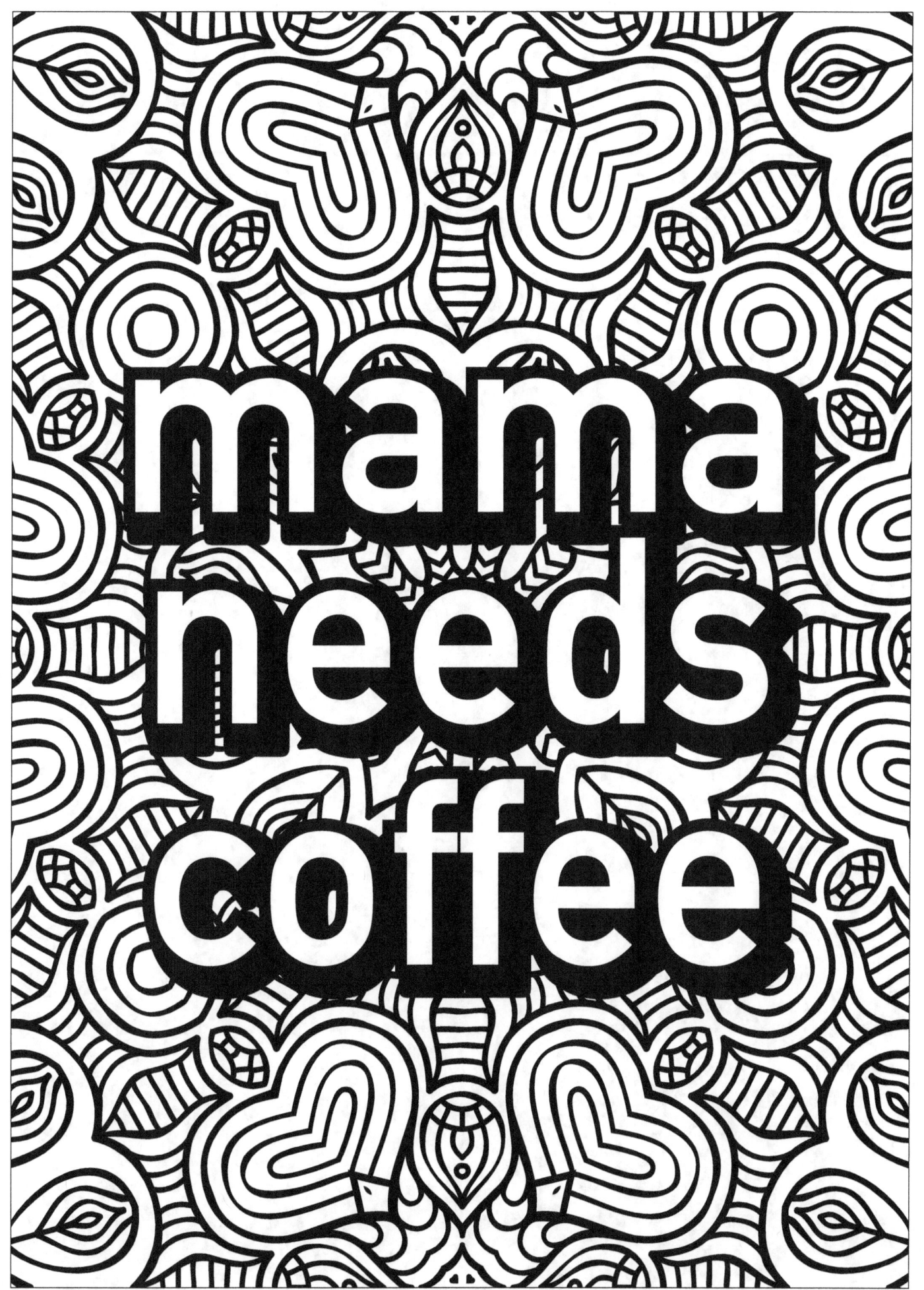

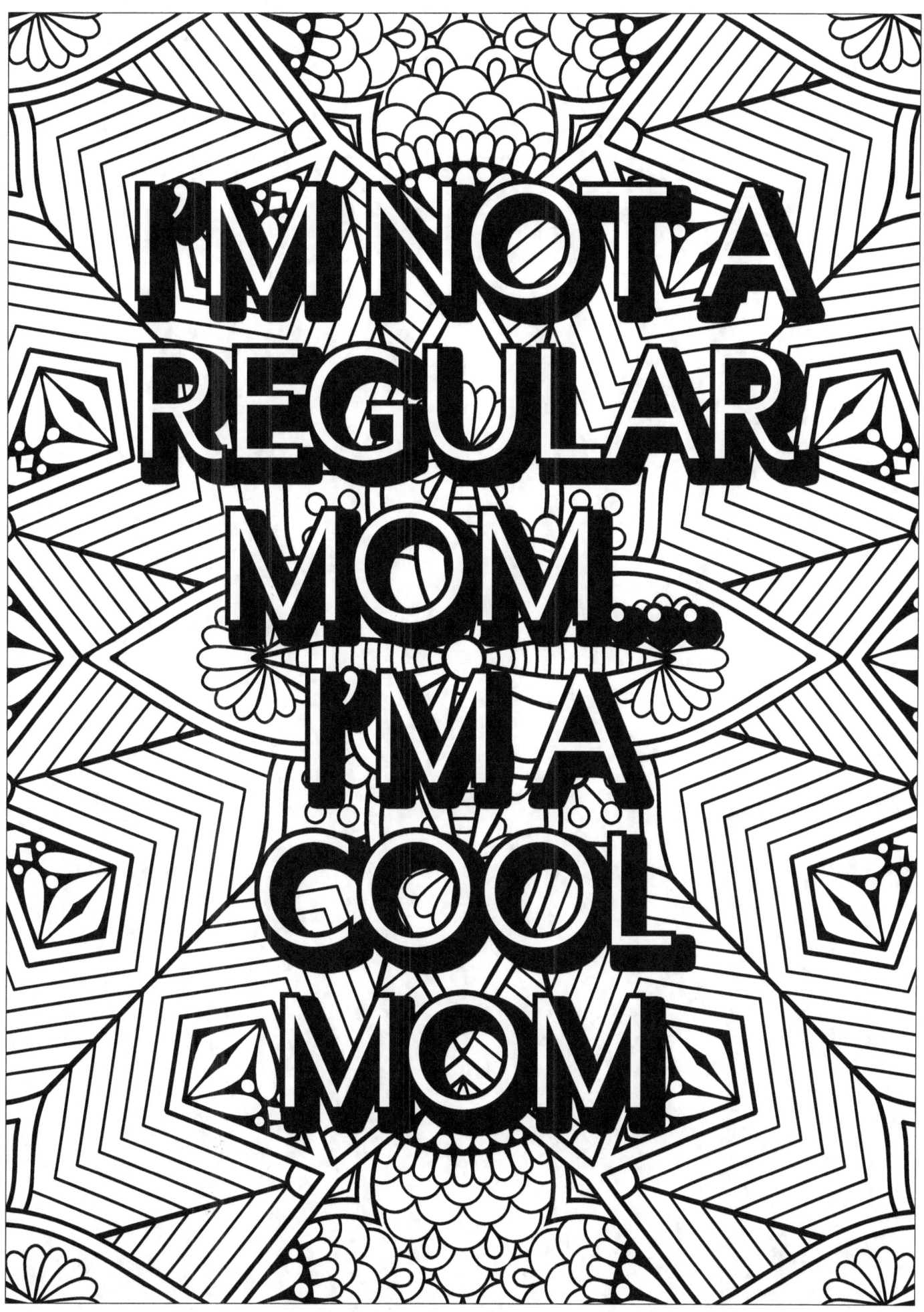

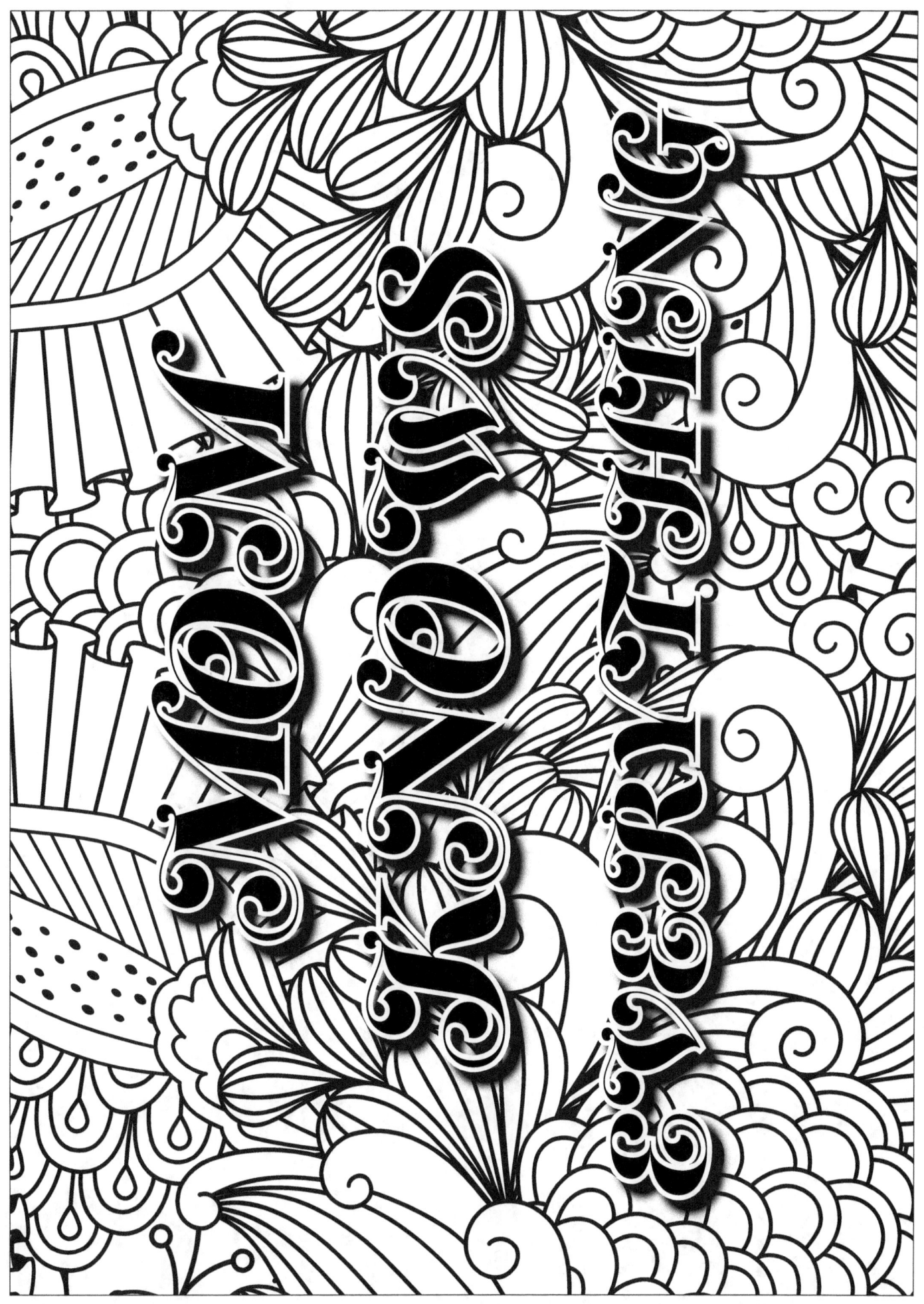

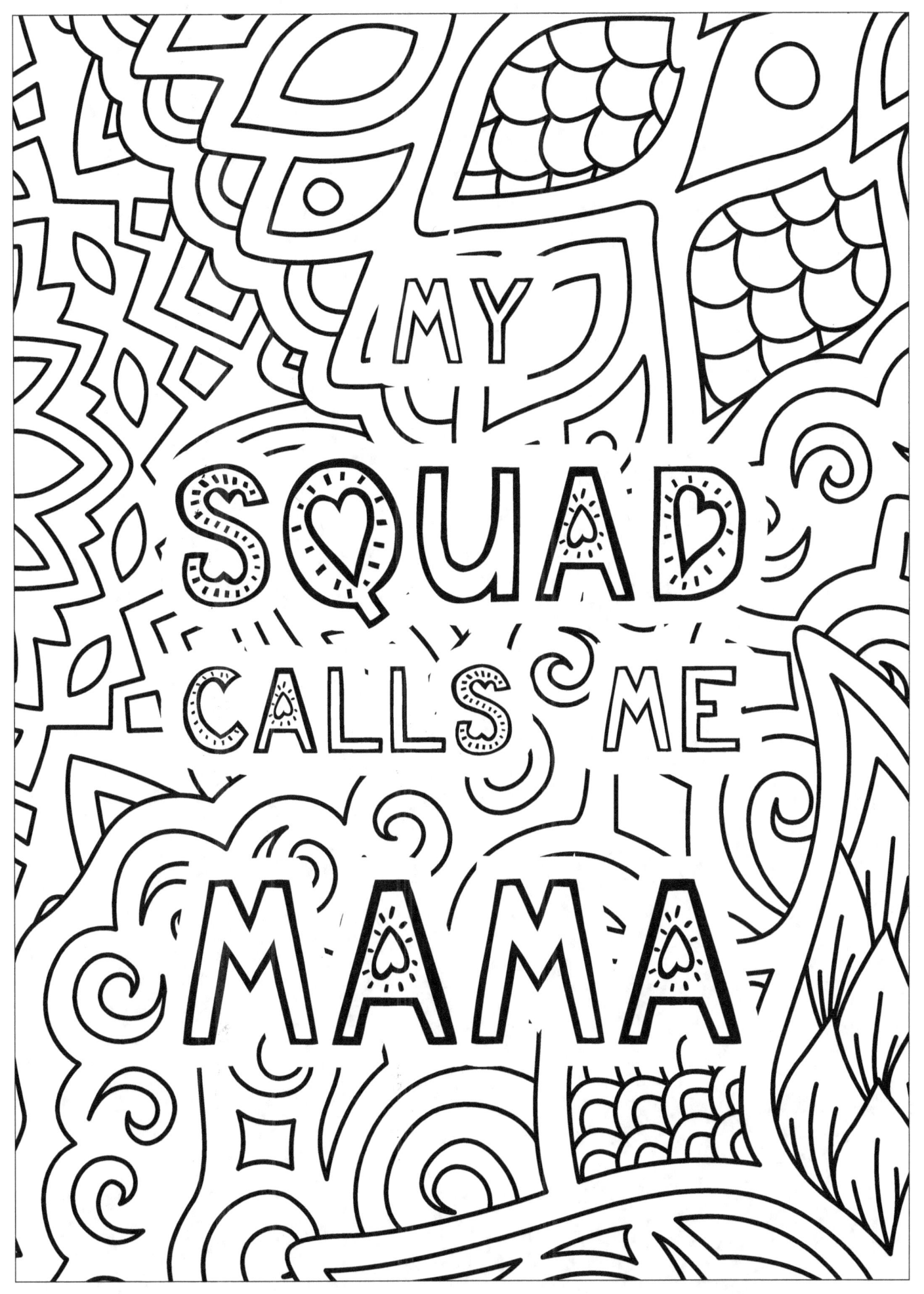

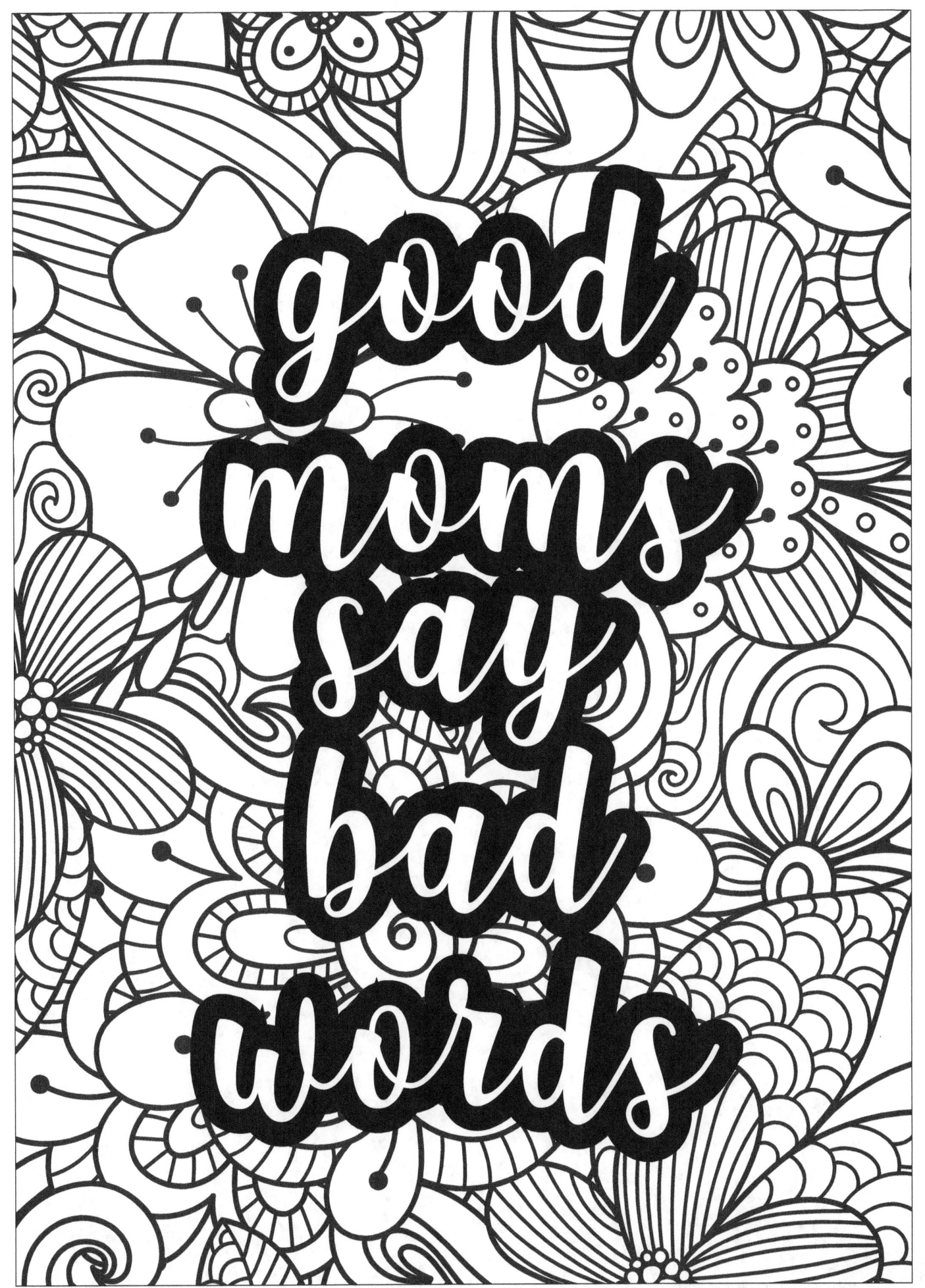